PRODIGAL PSALMS

D0104731

by

HARALD WYNDHAM

PRODIGAL PSALMS, by Harald Wyndham,
is published by Blue Scarab Press
in Pocatello, Idaho on November 1st, 1991.

ISBN Number: 0-937179-07-8

This book was printed for Blue Scarab Press by
LITHO PRINTING of Pocatello, Idaho

Address all correspondence to Blue Scarab Press
243 S. 8th Avenue, Pocatello, Idaho 83201

This book is dedicated

to the memory of Dr. Rhys Price

and to my friend, Thomas Witzel

for opening doors of the Spirit

and bringing the Living One

into my life

I no longer believe that God is up there,
and I don't believe that God is only within me,
and I don't believe that God is merely out there
      in history.

I think we are actually in God at all times.

— Madonna Kolbenschlag

Genesis 3: 22-24

Job 42: 1-6

Psalm 139

Luke 15: 10-32

It may be the devil, or it may be the Lord,
but you gotta serve somebody . . .

— Bob Dylan

1

O Living Being,
My only strength is you.
Alone, I am weak.

Wash me with your water, Lord.
Cool me with your deep running water.
Remove the burning voices,
the serpent at my ear,
coiled around my heart,
O drown him in your river, Lord,
wash him away like a withered vine
in the swift running stream of crystalline water
so that I am clean before you
like a smooth stone
polished by water.

Lady, Lady, you alone are my strength.
I call to you in my weakest hour.
Remove these whispering voices.
Burn them like thin grass,
like tall, dry weeds the fire celebrates
and the wind carries off in a whirlwind of ashes
leaving me empty and clean of desire,
that I may despise myself no longer,
but love the song of your voice
as it rises in my heart.

O Thou, you are my life.
Fierce fire, strong wind, cool water.
I surrender myself to your hand.
Be gentle with me.
Be merciful.

2

Lord, I am convinced that you are real.
You prove this to me time and again.
You never fail to give me what I need.
You work miracles in my own body.
You have restored the love I abandoned.

Do not desert me now.
I face the most subtle enemy — my own heart!
How vulnerable I am to its cravings.
Even in the night I hear its clever voice.
In careless moments it catches me off guard.

That is when I need you, Lord.
My own life is a testimony to your power.
Prove one more time how you save me,
how effortlessly you reach down
and cover me with your hand,
so the enemy cannot touch me,
so I hear nothing but stillness around me.

I am in the wilderness, Lord.
Feed me with rocks of silence.
Satisfy me with loaves of light.
Fill me with your spirit,
all day, all night.

3

O Thou,
How simple your presence is!

The sunlight fills the sky behind the trees
slowly, almost unnoticed, in early morning.

All appears to be still,
yet all is in motion.

Light increases every moment
moving through the garden, touching the flowers.

Move into my life in the same way.

Suffuse each inch and corner of my being
with your permanent presence, majestic as sunlight,
until each common part of me is aglow

and you rise in visible radiance
across my face.

4

How easily, O Lord, I turn away.
This morning I wake up weak and tired.
The last thought in my mind is to obey.
The tempter coils around me like a python
and I am too lethargic to give a damn.

O my true friend strengthen me even now!
Even at my worst, turn me around!
Put your hand inside me — touch my soul!
Steer me out of danger — I am blind.
Without your help I'll lose control.

Even in weakness, I submit and yield.
I wait upon you, O my strength and shield.

5

Lady, you are my keel and counterweight.
When I lean too far away, you pull me right.
When I run before the wind, you steer me straight.
Fastened in you, I cannot capsize.
Even in my sleep, you guide me.

How I am given over to arrogance.
Let me confess my mindless boasting,
blowing my voice around like empty chaff
while the kernels of ambition are winnowed away.
Thank you for curbing my careless tongue.
You provide me with constant mirrors.
My blemishes stand out like boils.
I stumble around like a blind man.

Lady, you are my counterweight and keel,
the fountainhead of everything that's real.

Thank you for being so deeply fixed in me.

6

Within your garden, Lord, I want to live.
The bees move steadily from flower to flower,
doing the task you have appointed them.
The trees stand tall and offer cooling shade,
the fruit trees hang pendulous with fruit
and every vegetable knows its place,
each bird its given song, each flower its bloom.
The insects work together at your will.
You raise your finger and the wind is still.
The clouds move peacefully across the sky.
The sun gives life to all, the lightfilled space
is changing, hour by hour, from dawn to dusk.

Only I seem useless. What is my task?

Let me be caretaker of this place.

7

How perfect is the universe you made,
requiring no additions or corrections.
I climb the mountainside to face the sun
and stand beside my brothers, the slender trees.
I know I am nothing, gone in an eyeblink,
save you fill me with the breath of life.

O Thou, how wonderful the morning light,
the radiant moisture moving between the trees,
the coolness in shadow, the wet grass,
and air perfumed with earthsmells, dark and green.
I raise my arms in the air and sing outloud —
how perfect is your glorious universe!

8

In the domed minaret of the flowering onion, Lady,
    I find you.

In the extravagant burst of the sunflower's golden brain,
    I find you.

In the common, tough, resilience of weeds and grass,
    I feel you.

In the expanding green shoots of the young fruit trees
    I discover you.

In the fat, red buddha of the half-buried beet,
    I touch you.

In the white, silken tassels of pollinated corn,
    I see you.

In the pungent, green tangle of moist tomato vines,
    I smell you.

In all hidden places, under crumbs of earth, beside stones,
    I uncover you.

Even at night, in the full moonlight washing the garden,
    I feel your presence.

O Gentle One, Friend and Nurturer, Mother of the Universe,
    you are everywhere.

Why am I startled to find you within my heart?

9

O Lord, I am made of doors.
    Open me and enter.

O Lady, I am made of windows.
    Penetrate me like sun.

All of my doors are locked, Lord.
    I am afraid.

All of my windows are curtained, Lady.
    I sit in the dark.

O burst open the doors of my heart!
Blow them from their hinges with your breath!

I will tear down the curtains myself!
I will stand and look you in the face!

O Thou, O Holy One, be merciful.
    Do not destroy me.

I stand, naked, open, waiting for you.
    I want no other.

Be present like cool fire around me,
    O Living Being,

    Father and Mother,
    O Lord, O Lady,

    Come.

10

I will sing out Thy connectedness through time and space!

Thou art everywhere alive, touching allthings at once!

Whoever I raise up in my prayer, you touch them instantly.

Even those who have died in the body, who are only spirit —

Even they are alive and strong in you — I know this!

How wonderful Thy mysterious infinite unfathomable presence!

O Thou unknown, nameless, Living Being of the Universe,

Whom I hunger for and love with all my heart.

11

Lady, forgive my ignorance.

Forgive my weakness in not trusting you.

Remove the debt I owe, before it overwhelms me.

I have no claim on anyone, Lady.   They are all free.

Forgive the part of me I hate, the darkness I once loved.

Transform my darkness, Lady, into radiance.

I am seeking you above all other things.

I am your child, your lover.

Lady, I have no other.

Be open to me.

12

How subtle the enemy is!
Sometimes he is so close to me
 I feel his voice is your voice.

This enemy made of infinite shadows,
 of tiny reasons and excuses,
 of just once exceptions,
 of words and wishes.

How can I defend against his treachery?

O cover me with your living armor.
It is light and easy to wear into battle.
 Nothing false can pierce it.

O cover my heart with hammered prayers,
 my head with the helmet of humility,
 my stomach with the shield of silence,
 my legs with firm bucklers of song.

Clothed in you, I am invulnerable.

13

How lovely morning is,
    the soft returning of daylight;
how joyfully all living things
    unfold their hidden faces to the sun.

I have lain in the fierce darkness
    have wrestled all night with demons.
I have feared for my very life
    like a lost child in an evil city.

Now your salvation is upon me
    strong as sunlight spread over the fields.
Now I rise up as from my deathbed,
    to sing your praises at the open window.

Lord, if you do not hold me through the night,
    how shall I live to see the morning light?

14

How thirsty I become
    when I do not drink regularly from your stream.

How parched and dry as desert sand
    when I do not soak my spirit in your fountain.

How baked and barren my heart
    scorched by desire for needless things.

How empty of all life I am, Lord,
    in this wilderness of my own choosing.

Ah, come to me now like summer rain!
Come in a cloudburst to quench my shriveled tongue.
Wash me all over with your healing water.
Cleanse me inside and out like a sacred cup.
Fill me with your liquid, living Word.
Let me drown and come to life like a marigold seed!

Like a seed that has lain in the earth
    for a thousand years
      let me be born.

15

Words of my mouth all false.
    I spit them out like pieces of dirt.

My tongue is my worst enemy,
    strutting naked and offensive on the stage.

What unkind thought will I not voice?
    What blasphemy not speak?

I who know nothing, am nothing, control
    nothing, create nothing, sustain nothing

Pretend to immortal vision, house of words,
    sand castle of syllables . . .

All the while your still, small voice
    is continually whispering:

    mercy . . . compassion . . . forgiveness . . .

You pass me continually in the faces of others '
    and I do not recognize you

Because I look only inward, listen to myself only,
    bombastic orator reciting in a vacuum.

And the great peace my heart desires, the bosom of love
    on which I long to lay down and be still,

Is as close as the grass under my feet, the smooth stone
    my hand rests on as I sit here unfulfilled.

Ah, Lady, why can't I just shut up and listen to you?
    Is it that difficult to be humble?

Touch my tongue with your fingers — teach me to be still.
    Put your lips to my ears and open them:

    forgiveness . . . compassion . . . mercy . . .

    Lady, I am waiting for your voice.

16

In Thou the great teachings unite.

What name shall I use to call Thee?

Yahweh, Buddha, Brahma, Allah, Wakantanka,

Great Spirit, Teacher of Righteousness, Father,

Mother, Fountain of Souls, Lord of the Universe,

The Way, The Suffering Servant, Ground of all Being . . .

Each of these is possible, and many others besides.

Those who are seeking you, find you somehow.

Those who would follow you discover the pathway.

From the heart of man comes deception and cleverness,

Injustice, cheating, falsehood, trickery, murder.

These have no existence except in our choosing them.

They are utterly foreign to your holiness.

You are a Being of Light, surrounding all darkness.

I call you Lord because I belong to you.

I call you Lady because you teach me to love.

I call you Thou, because you are present here.

O Thou, let me feel your Presence here.

Let me **know** that you know me.

17

God, but I am tired.

You are far from my mind.

I sit back, exhausted by the daily stream of events,
    crisis upon crisis demanding attention,
    wave after wave of petty obstacles,
    and the big emergencies screaming like sirens all night.
    How can I get any rest?

I look into each face anxiously, wondering
    what do you want from me?

I am too weary to be joyful about anything.

Come to me, Lord.   Come like cool, night air.

Fill me as a strong wind fills the trees,
    moving all their branches at once,
    shaking loose dead limbs and dry leaves.

Bring strong rain upon me, wash me down.
    Carry me away in the torrent for a few hours,
    sluice away the bitter dust of daily strife,
    that I may be lost to myself in you.

Take my responsibilities away for a few hours, Lord,
    so that I may walk in your sweet rain
    in the darkness of your lifegiving night
    and rest without fear, knowing you are
    taking care of everything for me.

Come, Deliverer.   My parched soul longs for you.

18

Think on the Unchanging One.

Think on this great creation
>   that moves to fixed laws in predictable rhythms
>   yet ever refreshes itself, is always renewed.

Think of the great generosity and love
>   that permits all beings to **COME FORTH!**
>   celebrating ten billion peculiar differences,
>   revelling in combinations of colors and textures,
>   each unique being an expression of holiness.

Think of the great laws of relationship
>   that insure the balancing of justice,
>   that reward faithfulness with love and life
>   and cheating dishonesty with isolation and death
>   as surely as atomic particles are bound and unbound
>   by strong and weak forces from time's beginning.

Think on yourself, your own color and texture,
>   think on your place in the weave of creation,
>   fixed in the pattern, stitched in this spot,
>   bound and unbound by choices made freely
>   in relationship with particular others,
>   all changing subtly hour by hour
>   as the great circle pulsates
>   to predictable rhythms
>   emitting light.

Think on the great Living Being,
>   curved and complete
>   centered in each point
>   containing allthings.

Think on the Unchanging One.

19

How heavy my burden seems.
I cry out despairing beneath it.
This discipline is more than I can bear.
The constant weight of it depresses me.
If I give in for a moment,
it will crush me to nothing.

Ah, Lord, you make all burdens light.
Uplift me now with your strong arm,
with your hand sustain my steps.
How easily you pull the hard yoke from my shoulder
and take it upon yourself for a time,
until I ask to have it set on me again
and steel myself to bear it best I can.

20

What do I know about anything? I do not even know
my own heart, or my future, or the day I will die.

Who am I to judge anyone? Am I the Lord?
Better for me to leave all souls to you.

O Thou, I am on my knees. Forgive my arrogance.

Break me like a wafer of crisp bread.
Crush me in your fingers like a cracker.

That I may be humbled, divided among many.
On my knees I pray for this, O Holy One.

21

Your branch in me grows strong and green,
 this branch of words
 with tongues of flame.

It was your gift to me at birth,
 your watermark
 staining my soul.

This branch grows with its own will,
 leading me forth
 into unknown places.

I serve it willingly without control.
 To force it
 is to break it.

Ah, Lady, be both the taproot under me
 and all the fruit
 hanging on the tree.

I would my own words fall away,
 dry syllables
 to crush underfoot.

Your words, only, Lady, will survive,
 like buds in spring:
 alive! alive!

22

In the morning, before the concerns of the day
    crowd in upon me,
Let me be still and fill my heart with your peace.

All things come from you.

And at midday, hurried by conflict and business,
    caught in surging traffic,
Let me stop a moment and lie down to rest under the trees.

All things abide in you.

At evening, as the cool air darkens around my head
    in the sanctuary of the garden,
Let me remember the generosity of your spirit.

All things return to you.

O Living One.

23

As the wind continually tests the strength of trees,
    the Lord tests us.

As the trees extend their branches into the air,
    we reach and grow.

In the quiet fullness of summer days, our pride
    stretches and flaunts itself.

Then the Lord comes like a storm wind driving rain
    and breaks off every branch
      that is not his.

24

Lord, you know my habits. I am loose
with language, yet each day I fight
for freedom of expression as if blasphemy
was my declaration of independence as a man.

My tongue is my destroyer — easy Judas! —
glistening like a serpent in my throat.
Glib and thoughtless, it fills me with death
like a shovel piling black dirt into a grave.

And you allow me to choose the best or worst,
chastening me with unresponsive silence.
If I wish to punish myself, I am free
to join the outer darkness with a curse.

Better, Lord, to cut my tongue at the root,
and be your servant, soundless, blind and mute.

25

Without your Word within me I am lost.

How easy, Lord, to avoid meeting you.
I am busy or tired or late for something or other.
I work and collapse, too exhausted to read.
And then it is days since I have opened your Word.

This is how he snares us away from you,
how hour by hour and day by day he distracts.
Events and busyness, firedrills unending
separate us from you like a freeway at rush-hour.

O Lord, let me always have time in the day
to open my heart and hear your Word for me.
There is no task more vital than this listening.
There is no person more crucial for me to meet.

Without your Word within me I am lost.

26

The morning light falls simply onto things,
    giving them form and detail,
    making clear their peculiarities,
so that all things shine from within,
    lit by their own, clear beauty.

Let daylight fall upon our faces, Lady.
    Bring us out of the shadow
    where nothing is clear or distinct,
where we blend together and disappear in a fog.
    Bring us into the morning light.

Let us look each other in the face
    and see the beauty of holiness
    shining from within.

27

Lord, take your rightful place within my heart.

What I would perform for the praise of others
    let me reserve for you,
    and do in your service.

Whether I be called to the center or sit on the sideline,
    take my anxiety away,
    restore your rich silence.

Remove all vanity from me, if that is possible.
    I am tired of my voice.
    I am hungry for yours.

Make me supple and accepting of whatever comes,
    branch in the wind,
    stone in the water.

Lord, take your rightful place within my heart.

28

O Thou,
be present with me.

Give me the patience of seeds
that lie for long years in the ground.
Help me keep faith in myself.

Give me the strength of grass,
to bend beneath pressure and spring back.
Help me hold on till tomorrow.

Give me the confidence of young oak trees,
who have no doubt of their potential.
Help me grip down and reach deep.

Give me the grace to grow slowly,
seeking the light and digging into the dark.
Help me be rooted in both worlds.

Give me the endurance of stones,
longsuffering children of eternity.
Help me lie down and keep still.

Give me a time and a place,
and contentment with what you provide.
Help me accept who I am.

Be present with me,
O Thou.

29

Hey, God — are you there?

I am lonesome and depressed.
No one chooses me or wants me.
I doubt seriously that life means anything.
Nothing gives me pleasure.
I have no appetite.
Even daylight filling the room tires me.

All my masks are abandoned.
Masks of language, dance and song,
large ritual masks of sexual power,
the terrifying mask of death with its crooked smile,
they lie on the floor around me.
I believe in nothing.
Even the love of others means nothing.
It is all a game, unreal, on the surface.
We do not know each other.
We only pretend to know.

I would be willing to die if it would prove anything.
I would die just to find out the answers to things.
By my own hand I would die if I had any ambition.
Yet even that is useless and boring to think about.

So what is there to do?

Wait for it to pass.
One day follows another and nothing lasts.
Tomorrow I will love you again
and believe you love me, too.
Today, I am hanging on.

So God — if you're there —
don't take any of this seriously.
Don't turn away from me now.
I need to talk to somebody
and you are the only one who will listen.

30

Lord, the flies are buzzing around my face.
    I cannot concentrate.
The enemy sends them to distract my prayers.

Lord, I will stop all this complaining.
    You know my needs.
You want only obedience, humility, acceptance.

I will defeat the enemy by thinking of nothing.
    I will sit in the sun for hours
letting your glory penetrate my face and skin.

I do not understand anything, Lord, for all my study.
    I am a little child before you.
I love what you are teaching me without words.

The enemy uses words like flies that tickle my ear.
    I am still as a flat stone in the sun.
You cover me with wind and watermusic drowning all time.

How long have we been on the earth together, you and I?
    This moment, the only moment.
There is nothing left inside me now but your voice.

Amen and amen.   Amen.
                        Amen.
                                Amen.

31

Lady, help my understanding.

There are great lessons
    in all the world religions.

The simple, single Truth
    lives in many voices.

Lady, why do we kill each other?

All who walk in peace
    walk with the Living Light.

All who practice charity
    are children of The Light.

Lady, why do we hate each other?

Our souls shine out,
    like candles in the dark.

You draw us to yourself,
    light to the Source of Light.

Lady, if you don't condemn us, who can?

Even the utterly lost,
    who have no Light in them,

Continually you are seeking,
    calling their names in the darkness.

Lady, let us live without judging.

Seek me and find me,
                Lady,
                      in that hour.

32

And when I am in the crucible, Lord,
    be Thou there with me.

Burn off my impurities with thy fire,
    the dross of things
    I cling to, works
    of my hands.

Smelt away my idolatrous imaginging,
    the hand-shaped goddess,
    beloved dancing
    fantasies.

Strip away all title, power and place,
    houses, riches, servants,
    illusions of importance
    and immortality.

Put my body into thy refining fire, Lord,
    assay my heart.

Whatever is corruptible burn away,
    dreams and ambitions,
    all my good intentions,
    consume to ashes,

leaving only a tiny bead of gold,
    refined and beautiful,
    perfect in your
    hand.

This is your truth in me, present
    from the beginning
    that cannot be
    destroyed.

For this I belong to you always,
    the chosen child,
    pearl of great
    price.

33

Be with me in my pain
    O Living One.

The enemy lives within
    my marrowbones.

He wrenches my bowels
    and crushes me.

He squeezes me empty
    of all breath.

I cry in agony
    and beg for death.

Hold me in your hand
    O Living One,

Remove the pain that rules
    my every thought,

Or else I do not want
    to be alive.

34

How easily I walk away from you.

I have been doing it all my life.

You wait for me, always, to return.

You have been waiting all my life.

It is arrogance makes me walk off,

a childish faith in your forgiveness.

I enjoy testing your infinite patience

as if it proves how much you love me.

Yet the wilderness will destroy me.

You have designed it to do so.

Only your garden will satisfy.

I know this although I deny it.

And now I hear voices of angels,

which are really the voices of demons.

Eat these stones, they command me.

Fling yourself down the escarpment.

Cry out to God and He'll catch you.

Stand up and be King of Nations.

Such a whirlwind of voices and ashes,

whirlwind of smoky ambitions.

And now at the edge of infinity

instead of oblivion — I find you!

You are here also — with me!

That is the ultimate mystery.

35

The husband waits by the window,
    watching for his wife to return.
    He bites his hand to keep from crying out.
    He knows she is deceiving him.

The parent sits up all night and waits.
    The child has not come home.
    Promises have been broken.
    Tides of anxious anger ebb and flow.

And you, O Living One, how grieved and disappointed,
    how justified in righteous anger,
    how hurt in not being chosen you must be
    by my unfaithfulness.

I have built a shack in the desert,
    far from your garden and temple,
    where I worship the work of my hands,
    surrender my soul to corruption
    dancing the naked totentanz.

How can I return after all this?
    How can I ask forgiveness?
    I have willingly betrayed you.
    I deserve the death I have chosen.

Yet I turn, O Living One, and call your name.
    In the dust of my foolishness I lie prostrate.
    Forgive me even though I deserve nothing.
    Erase all memory of my sin against you.

O Living One, I trust you utterly.
    Do not abandon me.
    Take me back as a servant.
    Give me a small room somewhere.
    Let me come home.

36

The enemy is strong against me, Lord.
He has already swept over my defenses.
He possesses the outer walls
    and lifts his scaling ladders against my heart.

What is my defense?
How can I stand against him?

He came against me in the night, when I was weak.
He had a betrayer open the door in the darkness.
He is utterly cunning against me
    and knows all the chinks in my armor.

And now he inhabits me.
The sound of his festival fills me.

O how can I survive this pestilence?
It is like I have locusts inside me,
and cockroaches swarming my courtyards
    devouring the last grains of faithfulness.

I sit in the tower you created for me
when light first broke in upon my world.

O Lord, the enemy wants everything.
Now he approaches the tower, my last refuge.
If you do not come now and protect me
    I will be overwhelmed and utterly devoured.

O Lord, I call upon you at this hour.
Deliver me from evil into light.

Restore me in health and power.
Drive the enemy from my gate.

Be my strength and sanctuary
And save me from the enemy.

I wait upon you, Lord.
Without you I am lost.

37

How quickly all I build is washed away,
    like a sandcastle when the tide comes in.
        One big wave and everything is gone.

My inner resolve to fast and worship you
    is washed away in an hour of sudden gorging.
        One mouthful and everything is lost.

Even that habit I have loathed for years
    comes back with a vengeance in this hour
        like black seaweed that stinks upon the beach.

Nothing that I build with my own willpower
    stands firm against the onslaught of temptation.
        Left to myself, I melt into desire.

O that you build in me your holy place
    footed on bedrock, mortared firm with grace
        stronger than imagination.

Then shall I survive the fiercest storm
    that piles wrecked ambitions on the rocks
        because your holiness inhabits me.

Then shall I not fear the undertow
    that drags me helpless into the dark below,
        because your holiness illumines me.

38

You know me, Lord —
    I am only human.
    The flesh that calls to me
    you made. Was that
    some kind of joke?

I love my appetites —
    though they seduce me.
    How eagerly I respond to
    hunger, thirst and that
    lovely impossible creature
    with the long legs.

The serpent lives with me —
    we are good buddies.
    Together we smoke cigarettes
    and drink forbidden wine.
    We tell each other stories
    long into the night.

So what is this command —
    to crucify the flesh?
    Why was I joined to darkness
    in the first place?
    Why am I always fighting
    against myself?

I do not understand —
    but I obey.
    The light I am wants union
    with your greater Light.
    What else will satisfy?

Grind it back to dust —
    whatever you will.
    The body is a place
    of beauty still,
    and spirit by itself
    is loneliness.

39

iwantiwantiwantiwantiwant

ineedineedineedineedineed

on center stage i dance i dance

watchmewatchmewatchme

o blessed one o favorite son

lovemelovemeloveme

dance prance smarty pants

the only only only one

igoyougohegoshego

egoegoegoego

another night another show

omomodadogod

dontgo

40

O let me sing the goodness of creation!
Let me celebrate the goodness of the body!

There is joy in simple health, Lord,
to lie in bed and watch the sunny sky,
wrapped in luxurious languor of a summer morning.

Then, in the backyard, on the perfect grass,
the autumn blueness bright as a morning glory,
I gather an armload of tomatoes in the garden.

Later, at midday, eating my lunch in the shade,
I know completely how good my body is,
how happily I live within this temple!

Why did you create senses if not to praise?
I bathe in perfect splendor in the perfumed air!
All of creation glows with your sensuous light.

Then, in the evening, out for a long walk,
I spin like a dancer under the first dim stars,
inhaling the moisture rising out of the earth.

O Lord, your presence fills me with delight!

41

O Thou, this day is perfect.

There is no need to wait until tomorrow.

This hour is time enough if I but listen.

This day is all I ask — it is sufficient.

Teach me how to be at peace with you.

Teach me how to celebrate all things.

Teach me how to be at peace with others.

I am open now and ready to receive.

O Thou Living One, be present here.

42

Slow me down, Lady, help me to listen.

I charge ahead bullheaded making my way,
missing the messages you left for me.

I injure others with my carelessness,
until your patient voice chastises me.

Still my anxieties, quiet my heart.
There is an amplitude of time available.

Prepare me for the encounters of this day,
that I may hear you and find you in each face.

Slow me down, Lady, give me to listen.

43

O Thou become in me a living flame,

a tongue of fire to dance across my face,

that I declare to all thy perfect name

and greet the lonely ones with thy embrace.

All I have learned I offer to thy will.

I want no other job than serving you.

O Thou consume me with compassionate zeal.

Give me honest, ordinary holy work to do.

Lead me among the lost, who suffer and cry.

Load me with poverty, hunger, anger and shame.

Send me into the darkness, to serve and die,

but do not abandon me, illumine my eyes

with the presence of thy paradise.

O Thou become in me a living flame

44

I cannot serve you while I serve myself.
Why do I turn away from you each day?
I cannot give myself what you can give.

And yet I am afraid to simply live,
trusting you to save me, come what may.
I cannot serve you while I serve myself.

Although I have acquired material wealth,
an hour's misfortune steals it all away.
I cannot give myself what you can give.

A lifetime passes through me like a sieve.
There are so many things I want to say!
I cannot serve you while I serve myself.

I worry constantly about my health,
as if by worrying I could gain a day.
I cannot give myself what you can give.

It is only by surrender that we live.
Possess me utterly, O Lord, I pray.
I cannot serve you while I serve myself.
I cannot give myself what you can give.

45

When I live without you, Lady, nothing changes.
 The sun comes up, goes down,
 The grass grows and is cut down,
 Leaves uncurl, fulfill and fall,
 wind and weather, rainfall, snowfall
 again and again, year after year
 while I get older here.

When I live without you, Lady, I am dead.
 I see nothing with new eyes,
 hear no new voice or sound,
 have no dance or song,
 encounter no new thought
 make no new friend.

When I live without you, Lady, life passes by.
 My children age and grow away,
 neighbors move in and move away,
 the household pets age and die,
 I suffer loss of ear and eye,
 withdraw into dumb solitude
 locked in frozen attitudes.

I have no life without you, Lady — come to me!
 Unsettle me with a touch of death,
 break my life apart and make it new,
 give me pain to dance to,
 and a great, risking love song,
 so that I bleed with rich wounds,
 and suffer every moment I am given.

Without you, Lady, living is not Being.

46

The Lord has invited me to his banquet —
    He has reserved a place for me at table,
    He has prepared room upon room for me to inhabit.

Why then do I arrogantly cling to this
    pitiful shack on the border of oblivion?

    Because I built it myself!
    Because it is mine — all mine!

I choose to be lord of this palace of sticks,
    ruler of snakes and scorpions.

In freedom I dance ragged and naked
    over my floor of dust
    in this pitiful birdnest mansion.

In freedom I sing glorious, heroic songs
    which the wind scatters in the night air.

And the Lord locks the doors to his house
    and closes all the windows
    and begins the great banquet without me.

47

O Thou
Here I am forty-five years old and still crying out
 like a two-year old afraid of the
  darkness around me.

O Thou, I am afraid of the darkness around me.
 I am caught in a nightmare trap.
  Please rescue me.

Even more than my mother and father loved me
 I know that you have always loved me
  and seek after me.

That is what keeps me alive in the wilderness,
 in this vicious, human arena
  surrounded by terror.

Your voice is a sweet song that sings me to sleep
 in spite of uncertain love and
  certain destruction.

Your name is a prayer on my lips even when I have
 fallen in with thieves and enemies
  who wish to destroy me.

I think of you all day and call your name all night
 knowing that you will never abandon me
  even as I am dying.

O Thou

48

In the night I walk into the mountains.

I climb to a high place just as the moon rises,

take off all my clothing and kneel on a stone.

The wind washes my body, stripping off masks.

I do not pretend to be important here.

Naked and vulnerable as any child of life,

I kneel on the gritty stone before your glory.

Moonlight soothes me with its gentle singing.

I listen for your voice coming out of the air.

O Lord, you have known me before I was born.

O Lady, I can never have secrets before you.

You are the great secret I have been seeking.

Reveal yourself in the tiny stones that dig into my knees.

Become visible to me as I am naked before you,

in the moonlight that touches the trees of the canyon,

in the cold wind that pulls the breath out of me.

I am waiting on you, O Thou, I will not leave.

You are the only one I have ever wanted to know.

You are the only song I have ever wanted to sing.

Let me die tonight if I cannot touch your Being

and be touched by you in all parts of what I am.

49

To Whom it May Concern:

Things are going to hell down here.

Homicide, rape and robbery are increasing.

Starvation threatens to go worldwide.

Half a dozen wars in process at once

and still the population explodes.

There's no room for all those other creatures,

the ones you created before you created us.

In twenty more years the whales will be extinct,

along with 800 species of tropical tree.

The air is sooty, the oceans filmed with oil,

fresh drinking water is hard to find.

It causes me to wonder sometimes —

Do you care? Are you there?

Is this all part of your master plan?

Or is it just the foolish fate of man,

with whom you are no longer concerned,

having turned your attention

to a new creation elsewhere?

Just wondering.

Sincerely,

The Red Clay Kid.

50

Now I am quieted down at last,

like an room empty of furniture

where the sun pours in through large windows,

filling me with a bright dancing stillness

and the shadows of leaves moved by the wind.

The terrible consequences have not come.

Somehow the ones I love survive catastrophe.

I do not understand, but I believe.

I know that you have blessed me.

Yes, yes, I say, with upturned hands,

The Living One has blessed me.

Amen. Amen.

51

Lady, we know each other.
Let there be no more disguises.
    I accept everything.

The bone beneath my skull declares
that I am already dry and empty,
    that I am history.

The rose in my heart insists
that nothing loved can be lost,
    that I am immortal.

You stand within me, Lady,
holding my skull and my heart
    in your hands.

52

Hold me back, Lord.
Let me not become a vulture.

The man lies fallen.
A thousand have risen against him.
Their anger is justified
and they pick him apart in their anger.

Let me be a kind hand lifting him up.
Let me be a encouraging word at his ear.
Let me bring comfort and forgiveness
and a loving, practical friendship.

It is easy to swoop down from on high.
Let me not become a vulture, Lord.

53

O Lord, I loathe the enemy in me . . .

> the sudden surging of self-righteous wrath
> that levels every bright soul in its path;
> the jealous worry that another being
> might upstage my performance in this scene;
> the tongue that dances like a naked sword
> decapitating rivals with sharp words;
> the anger bursting like a thunderstorm
> on wife and children who deserve no harm;
> the ego that demands its nobel prize
> without the suffering of sacrifice;
> the constant and voracious appetite
> obsessively devouring all in sight;
> the clever, calculating, wretched mind
> pretending to be gentle, loving, kind
> while working all the angles secretly
> to insure my own security . . .

Ah Lord, I love the enemy in me.

54

O Living Being,

be fully alive in me.

Come into all corners.

Inhabit my secret places.

Find me out and fill me.

Penetrate me with pure light.

Let me contain no darkness.

Drive out even the shadows.

O Living Being, inhabit me

so that I am nothing

but radiance.

55

There is no limit to your love for me.

Before I was born, you dreamed my face —
    you were there when the glistening sperm
    joined my father to my mother's egg
    and you sat beside me in her womb
    singing the pulsing lullaby.

You protected me from terrors I never knew —
    in all the climbing carelessness of youth
    your hand was with me to prevent my death,
    you healed my broken bones and saved my life
    ten thousand times from accident and malice,
    guarding me against my own stupidity.

You cared for me each day through hands of others,
    who fed and clothed me, gave me a safe home,
    healed my wounds and taught me to read,
    taught me their songs and stories of the past,
    and how to move gently, with compassion,
    with strength and speed at the critical moment.

You have pulled me from the pit of utter despair
    when I was lost to myself and lost my life.
    You saved my marriage and restored my wife,
    you gave us a place to live when there were none,
    and gave me a job when I had lost all hope.

Your miracles surround me every day!
    You intercede when I have screwed things up
    and turn my injuries into forgiveness.
    You have honored all the prayers I ever prayed
    and even when you send me sorrow and pain
    you never abandon me to suffer it alone.

I cannot doubt that you are Real,
    or when my body meets its death
    you will be there to receive my breath.
    Let me say it clear and sing it loud.
    You have been faithful to me, O Lord.

There is no limit to your love for me.

56

O Thou, I confess that I understand nothing.

I have studied at the University and have learned
to read and think, weigh, measure and assess,
processing experience into rational arguments —
yet I am overwhelmed by the inexplicable Universe.

The sun rises in the morning sky like a mystery.
The moon sets over the mountains — another mystery.
Who can explain the joy of walking in sunlight?
Or the excitement of a night sky blazing with stars?
Numbers and theories don't satisfy my longing
to **know** and **be known** by the Infinite.

And when the terror comes and my life is at risk,
when those I love are at risk and the world is ending,
what principal or philosophical truth
sustains me in my sorrow and calms my fears?
They fall away from me like paper clothing
and I stand naked with my hands outstretched.

I have seen the intricate inventions of humankind.
We continually worship the work of our hands,
as if gadgets and machinery could sustain us.
Always with our cleverness, comes violence,
always a polluting, corrupting, destructive ugliness.
Our medicines heal and our drugs addict,
our machines feed nations and destroy rainforests,
we have flown to the moon and polluted the oceans,
we have unlocked the atom and murdered millions.

O Thou, you alone attract, compel me.
You alone am I seeking and hungering after.
I cannot name you, control you, define you or own you
and so I continuously seek you in all things,
finding you most in the faces of other beings.
In the eyes of those I love you are revealed.
In the darkness behind the eyes I hear you sing.

O Thou, I confess that I understand nothing.

57

Great Mother, your presence surrounds me tonight.

In air freshened by mid-summer rain, your great aliveness
    wells up sweet and strong out of the grass.

Your constant concern for children who wander the earth,
    exiles, prodigals, seeking a lost homeland,

mingles with grief for the rape and abuse of all victims,
    grief for the wastage of uncherished beings.

Underneath sorrow, the abundance of life pouring forth
    in an unending stream, renewing, replenishing,

sounds a countertheme of driving, unstoppable voices
    redeeming and blessing all souls equally

in the great passion chorale of the double rainbow
    radiant against black thunderclouds.

Strong voices out of the earth, ancestral, primordial,
    lovers and warriors locked in the totentanz,

dance in bloodcell, chromosome, molecule, vibrating atom,
    taking in, giving off light at all levels,

so we are connected by filaments in fabric woven together
    like the many-colored coat of the universe

that covers your face, Great Mother, as you wander about
    seeking, distributing, finding, scattering

on harvest fields and battlefields, touching our faces
    and washing our wounds with your tears.

58

Lord, there are too many hungry.
    I don't know what to do for them.

And the naked and homeless are everywhere.
    Their plight overwhelms me.

On everyside, the pleading eyes of children,
    the wails of the abandoned,
    the cries of the tortured ones.

I want to turn my face, close my eyes,
    pretend they aren't there.

For I am the King's Son, beloved child,
    prince of a happy house,
    safe and protected.

How can I be happy, safe and protected
    while they are miserable?

How can I forget about their hunger,
    having seen their eyes?

59

Lady, for the last of the redwood trees,
    I light this candle.

This candle for the sycamore that I love,
    for the towering beech,
    for the supple birch,
    these candles.

I light a red candle, Lady, to remember
    a thousand acres of rainforest
    burned each hour.

For the bristlecone pine in the desert,
    asking for nothing but air,
    a small, green candle.

For linden, larch, red maple, apple and pear,
    blue spruce, fir and cedar,
    aspen and oak —

I touch my taper to the votive wicks,
    offering the flames,
    speaking the names
    like prayers.

How many prayers will it take, Lady,
    how many lights?

    One in every heart,
    ready to fight.

60

Nothing is Real except relationships.

We look out always for a face to find,
entering by permission through the eyes.

Without an audience, the windblown trees,
the towering mountains, desert and thundering seas
are dead scenery, unpraised and forlorn.

The universe is empty as atoms in space,
except we find creation in a face.

We meet and in that moment worlds are born,
stars explode and galaxies collide.
The impact of a friendship never dies.

The image of your face lives in my mind.
Your name will be the last word on my lips.

Nothing is Real except relationships.

61

Lord, I read the papers and despair.

    Governments collapse in civil war
    Mothers abandon their babies in garbage bags
    Boy slits woman's throat with his Scout knife
    Bus driver on drugs drives off a cliff
    Entire populations starve to death
    Prisoners and terrorists take hostages
    Jealous lover burns a nightclub down
    Bankers and stockbrokers steal millions
    Unemployed man opens fire with machine gun
    Dentist infects patients with AIDS virus
    Chemical plant blows up killing hundreds
    Gangs in cars shoot people on the street

All night these images disturb my sleep.

    Homeless wanderers carrying their bags of grief
    Prisons crowded with people jailed for life
    Children addicted to fantasies of murder and sex
    Smokestacks pouring pollution into the sky
    Supertankers leaking pollution into the sea
    Chainsaws and bulldozers clearcutting the forests

I did not make this world, but it is mine.

    I have always worked and paid my way.
    I have not murdered or stolen or cheated,
    or raped or rejoiced in cruelty to others.
    I have always tried to live responsibly,
    yet I participate in destruction every day.

Give me peace in my soul so I can sleep.

I think about the world, Lord, and I weep.

62

A word spoken in your name
    becomes Real.
    A curse destroys,
    A blessing heals.

Let all my words by thy words.
    Touch my lips
    with a coal
    from the high altar.

Let my tongue be thy tongue
    and thy kingdom
    be established
    in my heart.

63

Lady, I would be innocent again,

as in my youth before manhood began.

The enemy curled in me like a sleeping cat

and I ran free, not feeling the claws of desire.

When I was young, Lady, my love was true.

I was not afraid to speak with you.

I prayed sincerely, each night, on my knees,

and you were present in the room with me.

O let me throw away this adult mask.

The dance of sex I would not dance again,

but rather in a circle holding hands

with every soul that loves you I would sing

and move together as the spirit moves

in gentle patterns of harmonious concern,

each one serving and being waited on.

It does not matter what we claim to believe

or how we say we know you by what name.

It matters only how we choose to live,

and that we choose to bless and not destroy.

You know your children and when darkness comes

you call us by our names, each girl and boy.

64

My Father, how can I make peace with you?

Your stricture on me is too much to bear.

Thy bit between my teeth, thy rigid law

which, if I am to live, I must resist,

stands between us like a raised fist,

defining a distance I am bound to keep,

unable to approach you, unable

to touch and call you "Daddy"

like a little boy.

        It is lonely here,

far from your garden and vineyard,

in a wilderness of unhappy souls

who do not know my name or give a damn

if I die of hunger on the street.

I have wasted my inheritance.

But if I return . . .

            on my knees,

broken down and broken-hearted,

asking nothing but my daily bread,

will you run up with a joyful shout

and lift me to my feet and kiss my face,

forgiving all my foolishness and pride?

Or will you slam the door and turn me out?

Father, for fear of you I can't decide.

65

O Thou, I am so tiny — I am nothing —
a blade of grass amid a million blades,
one kernel in a thousand acres of wheat,
one face on a city street, one tiny stone —
how can you know and care for me alone?

I hide easily in my smallness here,
blending in without noise or motion,
overlooked and forgotten by everyone
until you pick me out from all the others
although I am unworthy — nothing at all! —
in your hand I am a precious jewel
exalted beyond all imagining.

66

Just as I choose the easy way,
    living careless, every day,
so I could choose by deed and word,
    to follow the footsteps of the Lord.

With every step, the choice is mine,
    to seek the common, or divine.
The easy way will get me lost,
    the narrow way leads to a cross.

Yet every heartbeat, every breath
    chooses perfect life — or death.
I fix my eyes on One who died,
    and urge my heart — decide! decide!

67

Today I just forget about it all.

The sun is shining and the wind is cool.

The trees are beautiful with light on them.

I am in health and at peace with all I know.

The world is between crises, quiet and calm.

Nobody that I care about is suffering.

The bills are paid, the chores are done.

I have not injured anyone.

There is time to just walk around.

There is time to BE.

Late in the evening, Lord, I realize

that all day I have been happy.

What a blessing that is.

Praise God.

68

I don't pray for money or success

    just let my children live

Give me an ordinary job, a modest home

    and let my children live

Forget all my ambitions and my dreams

    but let my children live

Lady, I only want one thing —

    let my children live

Let them live in fullness and in joy

    this girl, this boy

69

At my weakest moments, strength me.

When I am tired and irritable, relax me.

When I want to act out of anger, restrain me.

When I am about to forget myself, remind me.

When I am self-satisfied and arrogant, humble me.

When I am not listening, waken me.

Be with me all the hours of the day and night.

Take away my unceasing hungers, Lord.

Let me concentrate on you, instead.

Let my hunger lead me into brightness.

Allow me to be satisfied with little.

Allow me to eat modestly, without thinking.

Forgive my obsessive gobbling all in sight.

Break my habits, Lord, remove my lust.

Let me pass through violence into peace.

Let peace flow through me to other souls.

Let us sit together at your table.

Let us praise you as we break our bread.

Let us serve you as we serve each other.

70

Briar grow tall around me,
    cover my head;

protect my heart with thorns,
    keep the enemy out.

I would be safe from all desire,
    like a small animal
    in my nest of thorns.

★

O God, cover me with briar,
cover my body with spikes and needles;
let me be prickly as cactus,
keep the enemy from penetrating me.

I would be clean inside, untouched
as the clear water
in the heart of the cactus.

★

Great is your power, O God,
to cover my heart with bristles,
to protect me from the enemy.

Great is your mercy, O God,
to sit like a small bird amid thorns
and sing to me all night.

71

To smile at someone is a holy thing.

The face is open and the eyes are clear.

A friendly comment is a healing work.

Through such tiny graces we are saved,

esteemed and valued in another's eyes,

as if we were sons and daughters of the Universe.

What would it profit me to own the world

and live in isolate luxury afraid to move?

I am more blessed by a stranger's smile,

the handshake of my neighbor

and a laughing child.

When we know each other truly

we know God.

72

O Thou,

if appearances mattered at all
how could we survive?

The rich and famous cruise by in their yachts,
the violent lords of the street
cruise by in cadillacs.

if appearances mattered at all
how could we be brave?

Injustice rules by day and naked power by night.
The homeless, the widow, the orphan
have no advocate here.

if appearances mattered in the least
we would be crushed.

Children give birth to children they give away
as they were given away by parents
who are lost to themselves.

if appearances could be believed
who would have hope?

We worship glass and steel, power and combustion,
copper wire, instruments, alchemy,
things of our hands.

if appearances were reality
we would all die.

But we are alive
though we possess nothing,
we sing and we celebrate, we dance in your presence,
though we possess nothing,
yet we are alive
in our eyes and our souls,
in hearts unvanquished and spirits resurrected in love,
though we possess nothing,
we are very alive.

appearances vanish like scenery
revealing eternity
the brick wall
the mystery
and we stand before it singing
holy . . . holy . . .

73

When will that wildness in me burst forth
like a young colt — like a man gone mad in spring?

When will the rich fever in my bones
break through all reason and drive me away?

Lady, the guardian of the treasure sleeps —
the boy inside me wishes to go dancing.

What is your will for me? Must these wild dreams
pace like hopeless prisoners in my skull?

Touch my lips with a coal from the altar, Lady.
Give me wonderful, powerful, glorious words to say.

Give me pearls from the theologies of childhood,
and emeralds from before the beginning of time.

Let me swagger in the jewelry of imagination, Lady,
spreading your praise in spungold syllables.

Or let me run off into the wilderness like a horse,
without explanation, like a man gone mad in the spring.

74

Words are deceptive as serpents,
    slippery as snakes.

With words I say all manner of easy things:
    I love you above all others,
    I love my brothers,
    mankind, and so forth . . .

Windchimes of words bangle about in my brain,
    blown by big winds,
    hunger and war,
    hatred among peoples . . .

Words are condemning as commandments
    written in stone.

With words I relate to you, O God of Gods,
    with songs and psalms,
    with prayers and poems,
    with solemn testimony . . .

With words I deceive, condemn and cheat,
    with white and black lies,
    with empty promises,
    with careless curses . . .

Words are nothing, empty, pieces of air,
    whittled from cleverness.

O God, I am so tired of religious words,
    of visions and revelations,
    of prophesies and proverbs,
    of judgement and damnation . . .

I am tired also of all human statements,
    of scientific theories,
    of philosophic syllogisms,
    of cunning, rational explanations . . .

We live and die by the words we choose
    to live and die by.

O Living Word, abide in me unspoken,
    unspeakable.

75

So skillfully the armor is put on,
so gently shields lifted and spears thrown,
I scarcely recognize combat anymore —
the fierce look in the eyes,
the tense words, defenses set and anger pulsating
like a mad mosquito in the brain . . .

All those years of wargames,
dinner table, bedtime, daily chores,
the explanations, excuses and lies,
the awful, lonely aching to be free,
or justified or justly loved
without qualification — ah, Lord —
how quickly it returns to cover me
with heavy black armor when we fight . . .

I am so tired of justifying myself.
I throw myself down before you.
I am guilty. Yes. Yes. Yes.
Do what is fair and just.
Kill me if you must.
But I don't want to fight you anymore.
I don't want to lie.
I don't want to hurt anyone.

I am a sinner — yes.
A hypocrite — yes.
Reprobate — prodigal —
Unchanged — unchangeable —
Yes, yes, yes.
I am all this.

But I am also naked before you, Lord.

★

Sometimes her loneliness is
monumental
like an obelisk or a tomb
erected between us
and I cannot approach or speak
there are no words
appropriate
before such silence such
utter loneliness.

★

O Lady, healer of souls,
forgive me — forgive us both —
we are still children,
alone and sad,
wanting to be truly loved,
but fierce in our pride.
Honesty is brutal
yet we ache for an honest touch
and refuse all that is not
sincerely offered.

Lady, if you do not heal us —
who will?

★

The child in me —
still sucking his finger
in a dark room!

★

What good does it do
to study the scriptures
when your life is not changed?

How long can you teach
scriptures to others
when your life is sick and violent?

Your language violent.
Your discipline violent.
Your eating violent.
Your drinking violent.
Born of a love of this world.
Lusty with appetite.
Spurred by competitiveness.
Afraid of rejection.

And the peace of God
passes over you
unnoticed.

You are the ground
where the seed grows
quickly, only to die out
when trouble comes.

You don't survive testing.
You have no deep faith.
The enemy owns you
and all your talk is cheap.

Your son and daughter fear you.
Your wife is ashamed of you.
Your friends laugh at you —
you who pretend to be wise —
you who throw stones steeped in sin —
you whose hands reek with excrement —
you whose tongue drips filth.

★

Enough.

Strip off all masks.

Stand naked here.

> *you are nothing*
> *you have nothing*
> *confess.*
> *confess.*

O human creature.

Know yourself.

And be still.

★

(all is obvious and needs no explanation)

(everyone has eyes except you)

> *be still.*
> *be still.*

★

Serve — others.
Pray — constantly.
Speak — blessing.
Eat — simply.
Curse — never.
Strike — no one.
Desire — nothing.
Seek — peace.
Serve — others.

> *amen.*
> *amen.*

76

I have seen the face of evil.
    It is human.
    I am in its power.
    It enjoys hurting me
    as if I were a cockroach.

I have seen the face of God.
    It is human.
    I am free before it.
    It celebrates my being
    as if I were its favorite child.

Both these faces I have seen.
    In your face
    reflecting my face,
    reflecting the faces
    of our mothers and fathers.

77

O Lady when you touch us we ignite
like human candles with a radiant fire.

We give off beautiful, glowing light.
It is the spirit dancing in our eyes.

The untouched ones come to us in the night
out of the cold and isolate darkness.

We do not turn away — we stand upright.
The living flame passes from eye to eye

as for a breathless instant, we unite,
and step back undiminished, doubly blessed.

From us — mere candles — is the world made bright,
passing from soul to soul thy lovingkindness.

78

O joyous dance!
O light ineffable —
covering fields, illuminating trees —
filling the empty branches of my soul!

I dance before the Lord!
I sing and dance —
losing myself in celebration —
with no thought who might be watching!

O let me sing!
I cannot contain myself —
lift my arms over my head in the dance —
in music ecstatic in motion I sing and dance!

Here on this mountaintop!
As sunrise spreads across the open fields —
I know I am immortal — have always been your child —
Hosanna! Hosanna! Hosanna to the Lord!

I know there is no enemy!
All are one within you and before you —
all are dancing within me and without me —
there is one song, one dance, one earth, one sky!

O let me join you!
Take me into your glorious fields —
Lift me into the radiant realms of light —
let me be in this music, this dancing forever!
Let me shimmer in the spaces between atoms!
in the spaces between stars let me expand —
O light ineffable, O perfect
joyous dance!

Hosanna! Hosanna!
　　　　　　Hozoni! Hozoni!

　　　Hosanna to the Lord!

79

O Thou
even in the deathcamps abandoned
even in the bloody cells of military prisons
    suffering unspeakable torture
        you come to us

to those who are starving to death
to those neglected, uncared for
    who are too weak even to move
        you are available

to children abandoned by parents
to aged parents abandoned by children
    in cold, hollow places
        you appear

to those who stand at the abyss
who fall into a terrible decision
    who fall beyond hope
        into your arms

beyond what flesh can suffer
beyond what the mind can endure
    you are always present
        with us

they cannot drive you away
they cannot control or destroy
    what does not belong to them
        belongs to you

we belong to you with or without our bodies
without our minds driven mad by torture
    your song sings in our hearts
        we know your voice

we come to you through a veil torn in the flesh
through a doorway that suffering opens
    we enter the bright cloud
        of your presence

halleluhia! halleluhia! O let us praise and sing!
the doorway that suffering opens cannot be closed!
    sing halleluhia O my soul
        and enter in!

80

And when we die,
    O Thou be kind to us.

When the flesh crumbles away
    and we enter the place
    prepared for us

    O Thou be present there

We cannot guess/we do not know
    what place, what it can be
    if light or dark or
    emptiness or joy —

    and so we fear it

O Thou be kind to us in death
    we come as children
    each of us alone
    afraid of the dark
    seeking a loving brightness

O wash us in merciful light
    healing all wounds,
    removing all burdens,
    and clothe us in peace,
    answer all our questions,
    and sing the ancient lullaby
    until we fall asleep in your arms

    O Thou mystery of mysteries

    O Thou destination

    O Thou city of singing souls

    Receive the prodigal.

81

In hunger we are rich
    O Holy One

Thou born of the thorn bush
    petal upon petal
    concealing
    mystery

Thy crown of thorns conceals
    rich petals
    of pain

In sorrow we are hungry
    for thy body
    broken for
    thy blood

This ugly splintered tree
    of spikes and
    thorns a scarlet
    blossom bears

    Thy Name

    O Holy One

    O Sealed Buddha

    O Rose of Jesse

See we take hands and dance
    in a circle
    around
    you

82

Scour me clean, O Lord,
    inside and out
        like a golden chalice.

Remove the poison from my blood,
    the meat from my bowels,
        the fat from my bones.

Scour each syllable,
    scrape me of appetite,
        rinse away my obsessions.

Sift every thought
    and winnow my words
        of all cleverness.

I would be thy
    dwelling place,
        O Lord of Truth.

Open the windows
    and let wind inhabit me
        and the birds of thy Spirit
    let them roost in my skull
and sing incessantly.

83

and the great liberation we tasted
    grows tiresome

the great sexual freedom we explored
    has petered out

i never thought i'd see another
    butch haircut

or baggy trousers and my father's shirts
    in fashion again

the great atheism, like communism,
    has collapsed

and everyone's a believer
    once again

Reality is moral, not empirical,
    and the Truth

is what we make of it, a matter
    of choosing

i choose Jesus, you nirvana, him
    mantra, she

astrology, them biochemistry &
    it's okay, see?

science is another way of seeing
    like religion

and all that really matters is
    you & me, baby

raising our kids the DNA way
    naturally

on this blue green speck of
    stellar dust

part of the process cradle
    to grave

    BURMA SHAVE

84

and if it is simply death
without fanfare,
    without rapture or
        resurrection,
    without heaven or hell,
stiff, still, nonbreathing, nonbeating
nonbeing, inconceivable nothingness, well

    so be it, Lord.

it's your creation, after all.
i am just here,
    making nothing happen,
        ephemeral,
    creature of a few hours,
and everything i think, create and feel
lasts no longer than snowbanks or spring flowers

    so be it Lord.

my dream of you, my dream
of my own life
    is still an honest dream,
        beautiful
    as a violin concerto,
taj mahal, pyramid, pythagorian theorem,
prayer wheel, tapestry, sunflowers by van gogh

    so be it, Lord.

i cannot second guess
your perfect word
    nor refute the arguments
        of scientists,
    philosophers, agnostics, atheists
who have created realities of numbers and words
proving to 99 percent probability you don't exist

    so be it, Lord.

i struggle in this life
with my poor power
    restricted to one viewpoint
        imperfect
    distorted, limited in scope
by history, genetics, sensation, desire,
and yet, for all that, unlimited in hope

    so be it, Lord.

85

and if under stress
of poverty or pain
i pull away from you
curse and deny you
give up all faith
confess to lies
accept nothingness
abandon hope
and wander into
a godless wilderness
at gunpoint or
grief or sorrow
coerced by argument
out of weariness
or because i am weak
and the enemy clever
because life bewilders
paradoxical, immoral
and hypocrites abound
and the wicked prosper
and televangelists deceive
and science confounds
and everyone believes
and what do i know?
it all seems pointless
there are no answers
in telescopes microscopes
big bang to quark theory
abortion to nuclear war
where are you anyway?
are you dead?
do you care?

if i abandon you

O Thou do not abandon me

remember the prodigal

receive me, forgive me

never stop seeking me

O Thou my only hope

86

The enemy is a sly companion, Lord.

He catches me off guard when I am feeling good,
    in quiet, desert places,
    in careless moments.

Sometimes while kayaking from rock to rock
    amid the whirlpools
    and daily dangers,

I forget you are the river I am riding on.

Then let your voice cut through the blur of the day.

When I am most preoccupied, be suddenly with me.

87

I am like a child who asks for a gift
    and runs away to hide when it comes.
Lord, do I fear your power so much?
    Am I so arrogant to test you?

The spirit in me pushes me to ask.
    The child in me hides, afraid to take.
The man lacks courage to receive,
    afraid of the changes you will make.

You changed me once, Lord, overnight.
    I know your power is great.
I would be free of lust and clean as air.
    I kneel naked and impoverished before you.

For I belong to you, Lord, bought and paid.
    I stand abandoned, locked-up till you come.
O enter me like the owner of the house —
    Light the lamps again and live in me!

88

For thy miracles and lovingkindness, Lady,
   I give thanks this morning of my birth.

For forty-five years in the body without disease,
   all parts functioning, nerves, synapses, tiny
   tubules, blood vessels, bladder, bowels, hands,
   teeth, eyes, brain, lungs, stomach, arms, legs
   manipulative fingers, toes, tiny hairs in my nose,
   ear drum, pituitary, thymus, tongue and heart —
   I give thanks this morning of my birth.

For love received and given away so that I am not alone
   with family wife children friends relatives
   living and dead surrounding me always connecting me
   to mankind to creatures back to the first molecule —
   I give thanks this morning of my birth.

For peace among peoples, for freedom in my lifetime,
   for work and opportunity and shelter and food,
   all undeserved, unearned, enjoyed without thinking,
   for the creative urge expressing itself freely
   without persecution or fear in a free country —
   I give thanks this morning of my birth.

For your love, Lady, which at all times surrounds me
   like a blanket of light, protecting me, touching me,
   providing more than I know to ask and in abundance,
   despite my ignorance and deliberate offenses,
   ten thousand thoughtless failings all forgiven —
   I give thanks this morning of my birth.

For allowing me to come into your presence,
   into your beautiful universe,
   into your holiness,
   O Lady, Almighty and Perfect Mother
      O Living Being —

   For sustaining all my days upon the earth,
   I thank you on this morning of my birth.

89

Now I bring you forward for a moment
    like a little plaster saint
    from the locked cupboard

Now I light the candles and say the prayers
    remembering for a moment
    those I have injured

Now I swing the jar of smoking incense
    once in each direction
    remembering the poor

Now I sing the hymns and chant the creeds
    staring out the window
    at birds in the trees

Now I rise and put you in the cupboard
    back where you belong
    until next sunday

Now I go out into the world of men
    do my dirty business
    once again

90

i cry out to you from the abyss

we slaughter each other every day
    for love, for land
    for money and lust
    for justice and peace
    for slogans and principals
    for this god or that god
    in the streets and in our homes
    in wars, terrorist acts, reprisals
    in concentration camps
    in political prisons
    with righteous anger
    without humility
    without tears

i take part in this daily murdering
    with every bite of food
    with every drop of water
    with every comfortable breath
    with silence and assent
    without protest
    without risk

O let me believe in no god or power
    that demands murder
    that encourages torture
    that calls killing justice
    and war peacemaking

let me ignore all theologies
    don't tell me what you believe
    show me how you live!
    what do you choose?
    who are you serving?
    what will you die for?
    can you resist violence?
    can you suffer instead of striking?

and when i turn this catechism on myself
    i am found wanting
    a failure on all counts
    lacking courage to act

Spirit, give me courage to respond
    to serve and act
    to risk my life
    living the Word
    healing the world

91

O Thou

I know your followers abound
    heaven and earth
    are full of your glory
    you are not defeated

I am surrounded by believers
    sensitive and tender
    courageous and strong
    who serve you daily

You know neither race nor creed
    you see us as we are
    beyond language
    without politics

Darkness tempts me to despair
    I see the injustice
    I feel the suffering
    I forget your healing

Forgive me this lack of faith
    standing isolate
    wringing my hands
    without community

Draw me back into the circle
    body of believers
    suffering servants
    joyous celebrants

Even in death let me see you
    in each kind face
    each generous act
    each free gift

Let me join the circle of believers
    at work in the world
    healing, sustaining
    joyous and praising

O Thou

92

O Living One

You reach out and touch us
and we glow

You lift up and magnify us
individually

You give us impossible tasks
and amazing strength

You challenge us beyond capability
and provide a way

With You we have moved mountains
and crossed oceans

With You the desert yields fruit
the sick are healed

For each of us the power of the Universe
is close at hand

Overwhelmed, we cry out for help
and find You

You prove your faithfulness to us
in every hour

Not to conquer or dominate or win
some human goal

But to have us learn who we are
and who You are

So we may live abundantly together
without fear

O Living One

93

We must resist evil, Lady,
    however we can.

We must not promote violence
    in speech
    in prejudice
    in jokes and jibes
    in murder and rape.

We must not back down and turn away
    but stand face to face
    with the enemy
    resist and suffer
    work against in all ways
    be willing to die.

All this with gentleness, Lady,
    with love in our eyes
    seeing beneath anger
    hoping beyond hatred
    to the vulnerable soul
    the battered child
    the abused animal.

I say this and believe it, Lady,
    but every day I fail
    out of fear for my life
    courage melted away
    in face of consequences
    tanks, machine guns
    threats in the night
    death squads, reprisals
    brutality in all forms.

Forgive me and help me, Lady.
    Let today's failure
    strengthen tomorrow.
    Let me back down
    only to come back again.
    Do not forsake me.
    Give me another chance.
    So I am not beaten
    and gathered in by cowardice.

Teach me to forfeit my safety, Lady,
    in daily defiance of evil
    like the murdered sisters
    like the martyred brothers
    like Children of Light who are everywhere.

94

O Living One

Your will is always for freedom

LET MY PEOPLE GO!

Our will is to dominate each other

LET MY PEOPLE GO!

You are the hope of the captive
    the beaten wife
    the abused child
    the prisoner
    the slave

You are the enemy of tyrants
    unsleeping rage
    sparking rebellion
    in sullen eyes

At the end of this bloody century
    in Europe, in Russia
    the walls torn down
    empire collapsing

LET MY PEOPLE GO!

In South Africa an end to apartheid

LET MY PEOPLE GO!

Church bells and dancers in the streets

O Living One

95

Lady, hear my voice.

I have no right or authority.

I have no title, position or power.

I am a prodigal, one of your wandering children.

I have wandered away from the churches.

The priests and the pitchmen depress me.

The hymns and the promises seem pale.

Everyone has the wrong answers.

People are thrown away empty.

Children are crushed underfoot.

Technology rules like a tin god

and everyone bows to the dollar.

I raise up these psalms in despair.

I have nothing else to believe in.

The skeptics will cut them to ribbons.

The expert theologians will snicker.

The rich and the powerful will scorn them.

Perhaps the children will listen.

Perhaps they will not.

O Lady,

Perhaps you will listen.

Raise up a house for the prodigals,

a sanctuary for outsiders and misfits,

where any are welcome without explanation,

and the only password is prayer.

96

Lord, I made all the wrong choices.

Your gift of love, this bright soul
    opened for me to enjoy
    in divine lovemaking
    instead I am thinking
    of the next beauty behind her

The child of love we created
    scared me to death
    I ran away from it
    let the mother decide
    if it lives or dies
    this bright soul out of our bodies

I am the betrayer, thief in the night
    untrustworthy, devious
    sneaking and cheating
    dogged by my demons
    damning the consequences
    squandering life like cheap money

Darkness inhabits me, chemical nightmares
    evil in all forms imaginable
    screams on the screen
    sexual perversion, pornography
    anything forbidden, obscene
    nakedness, ugliness, high volume violence

None of it satisfies, leads nowhere:
    this empty room, blank wall
    old hotel, jail cell
    nameless, faceless
    no one to give a damn
    a stiff for the county to bury

Too late to change anything, Lord
    all of it's ruined
    freely, unforced
    against all advice
    in spite of all prayers
    I screwed it up on purpose
    just to show who's the boss

Ah, Lord, I'm sick of my choices.
    If there's anything left
    give me one more chance.
    You lead this time.

97

O Mother help me
decide how to live
with this child
or without it
i am so afraid
yet i want it
one minute dont
want it the next
like a trap it
clamps me tight
i have no life
with this child
no future without
it no lover i
want to be free
but i want it
to be happy
like i am not
happy O Mother
help me decide
what to do it
is real deadly
serious up to
me to choose
how can i
follow my
heartbeat
my heart
mother
help

98

no one love me this i know

cause my hunger tell me so

people come and people go

i don't have no place to go

yes no one love me

yes no one love me

yes no one love me

my hunger tell me so

99

Well God, they say you are dead.
 We have outgrown the need of you.
 We have empirically proven your absence.
 We are getting along fine without you.
 The Number has replaced the Person.
 Nobody cares about you anymore,
  so they say.

Yes God, we have achieved miracles.
 We fly faster and higher than eagles.
 We have wiped out malicious diseases.
 We speak on polished beams of light.
 We have dissected the atom.
 We have decoded life's secret.
 We have walked on the moon.
 All in the last hundred years,
  ain't it wonderful?

But God, our violence increases.
 We have murdered millions.
 We have world wars and deathcamps.
 We have turned miracles into weapons.
 We have decimated whole species.
 We have polluted the planet.
 We have abandoned each other.
 We have mass starvation.
 All in this same hundred years,
  ain't it terrible?

So God, if you don't exist, what are we?
 Our cleverness traps us.
 Our greed outstrips sanity.
 Our free choice deceives us.
 Our technology separates us.
 Our entertainments diminish us.
 If you don't exist, we will have
  to invent you.

Lord, Lady, Living Being, Rose of the Universe
 ever present and suffering
 in all things,

  reveal yourself
  mysteriously
  alive.

100

Let us praise the Living One together.

Let us sit down at one table and take hands.

Let all weapons, hungers and hatreds be laid down.

Let men and women of all races sit down together.

Let us share a common meal with our brothers and sisters.

Let us forgive and be forgiven at the table of Allah.

Let us give and receive mercy at the table of Krishna.

Let us be tolerant of each other at the table of Buddha.

Let us make room for each other at the table of Yahweh.

Let us serve one another at the table of Jesus.

Let us remember one another at the table of Ancestors.

Let us honor all creatures at the table of the Great Spirit.

Let us rejoice in knowledge at the table of Imagination.

Let us share a common humility and hunger for love.

Let us make room for the outcast and the untouchable.

Let us celebrate the return of the prodigal.

Let us pray for those who will not come.

Let us celebrate our differences.

Let us live in tolerance of each other.

Let us pray with one voice the many names of God.

O Living One, bring peace to all gathered here,

peace to all peoples, peace to the beautiful earth,

empower us with your Spirit to love each other,

and to be good stewards of the sacred land.

We ask this in the Name of Names. Amen.

101

Kaleidoscope of faces constantly turning

Mandala of relationships fixed in time

Great prayer wheel of reincarnation

Sandpainting of the four dimensions

Great calendar of all possibilities

Starwheel of seasons laid out in stone

Pyramid preserving the perfect idea

Sun, moon, fixed stars of the zodiac

Cabala connecting seen to unseen

Deoxyribonucleic acid —

O hear us!

We dance to drum and flute, rattle and stick,

in ritual circles as the heavens turn,

looking upward, inward and outward for a sign.

What do all these layered patterns mean?

Why did you take such care creating them?

How can learning them preserve our lives?

Speak, O Sacred Ones, explain yourselves.

These dancing specks of dust demand to know.

102

and after so many years
talking to you like this
it is inconceivable
that you do not exist
o friend, no one else
has been with me
from the beginning
seen everything
good and bad
delivered
when i needed
salvation of all
kinds, houses, jobs,
intercession, healing,
comfort and courage
someone to write
poems for, audience
for all seasons
companion in
dark places
and mountain peaks
you understand everything
i feel nothing is
hidden from you
i must be honest always
even when i lie
you find me
lover
i cannot doubt
your presence here
before and after
inside/outside
alpha/omega
world
without end
amen.

103

Lord, what can I say?

The food harlot touched me with her greasy hands.

I melted in her fingers and gobbled with greed.

For hours she rode me bareback through the house.

I did not want it, yet I wanted it.

Forgive my obsessive, human appetite.

Tomorrow I will shower and take a long walk.

Tomorrow I will fast and pray all day.

Tomorrow I will be yours again.

Today . . .

104

Lady, you only wish good things for me,

yet the world reaches out with its hooks

and sometimes everything goes crazy

like cars spinning out of control on the freeway

and we pick up the pieces afterward best we can.

Lady, you do not wish catastrophe,

yet the world is a messy place,

spinning off-balance with wild emotion

and in the heat of the moment I say things,

make bad decisions, step off the edge

and there is nothing you can do but watch

and come back later to patch things up.

Lady, I don't blame you for my problems.

Things would have gone better if I had listened.

I just praise you for not turning away,

for suffering with me and with the world,

for loving me in spite of my arrogance.

I'm a fool, but you are wonderful.

105

Creator of faces!
Such a great work you have done!

They surround me on all sides,
young faces, old faces, men, women, children,
white faces, yellow faces, red, black, brown,
some with bright eyes and glistening teeth,
others with shining hair and eager smiles,
others angry and sullen, full of emotion,
the faces of lovers like candleflames,
an avenue of faces in motion
like sands of the ocean.

They are all faces that I love,
although I do not know any of their names.
I love them because they are human and beautiful,
because I belong here, in the midst of them,
with my own particular, strange face,
my bright eyes, eager smile.

How you must delight in seeing them,
these colorful wild flowers by the roadside,
all looking up to the source of light,
hopeful and expectant,
beautiful faces.

What a fine piece of work they are,
O Creator of faces!

106

And when our bright ones die, what can we say?

No words can fill the emptiness they left.

It's not that we blame you for taking them away.

We understand the capriciousness of death.

But these! Why these? Why now?

We ache collapsing inward with our grief,

shocked with sorrow and with disbelief.

They were the foundation of our lives.

Our only purpose was to help them grow.

Were it still possible, we'd sacrifice

everything we have that they might live —

our very bodies, organs, blood and heart —

offered freely and without a thought.

Instead, we take what comfort prayer can give

and lean against each other in the dark.

Our bright ones taken from us — O dear God —

be mother and be father to them now.

107

Lady, fill me now as the barren trees
are filled in early spring with opening buds.

All your gifts are sealed in my branches.
Bring sunshine and warm rain into my life.

Swell my buds, burst my tight-fisted heart.
Let blessings and blossoms explode on every side.

That I may be loaded down with life for others,
kindness, prayers that open a billion petals.

Lady, fill me now with opening buds,
as barren trees are filled in early spring.

108

I am astounded by each thing I see,
the intricate detail down to the finest hair,
grain within grain, structure of color and light,
all of it holding together perfectly.

I turn a scarlet maple leaf in my hand.
The veins that subdivide off the primary stem
are further subdivided again and again
down to the cell, the molecule and atom.

I myself am another collection of atoms,
held together by the same chemical force
that binds the outer edges of the universe.
Such unity is more than I can fathom.

O let me always explore, but never pretend
that I am anything more than a mortal man.

109

Let my heart be a bush filled with birds
    a lilac bush in winter
    crowded with sparrows,
sheltering, containing so many prayers
for those I know who need your love dear God.
    Let me hold them in my heart
    like a bush full of sparrows
not one of which falls to earth unnoticed.
These tiny ones crowding in upon my heart,
    let me hold them in prayer
    while you feed them, Lord,
these tiny sparrows shivering on the branches.

★

Lord I would be a sparrow
sheltering in the branches
of your spreading mercy

★

Anxieties gather like sparrows
perched on twigs in my heart
gossiping about the future.

Then the Lord comes and
WHOOSH! they lift and scatter
and I am filled with nothing but light.

110

Lady, pray for all prodigals.

Far from you we wander,
searching for happiness,
holding on to each other
or drifting apart,
until we cannot remember
your voice, the way home,
we call out to anyone,
shelter in caves,
savagely fight
to eat, to live,
forgetting how to love,
lost in our hungers,
children abandoned
abandoning our children,
worshiping rocks,
carved sticks, things
of our own making,
unsatisfied,
searching always
for what we forgot,
the pathway to silence,
inner quietness,
light of the soul,
gentleness, the open
hand and heart,
motherlove,
freedom to BE.

We do not even know
who we are crying for
in the night.

Have mercy, Lady,
and be present here.

III

O Bread of life,
    be nourishment to us.

Bread of many forms,
    flat, raised, rolled, baked on stones,
    crisp, soft, textured, whole grained,
    brown, white, golden, red and black,
    be nourishment to us.

Single Bread divided,
    passed from hand to hand to be torn,
    broken, snapped, sliced, ripped, bitten off,
    from mouth to mouth among mankind
    be nourishment to us.

Holy manna, heavenly food,
    in all languages we know and praise you,
    in all prayers we ask for you each day,
    in all homes you live with us,
    feeding body and soul.

Bread of the earth,
    Let baking be our vocation,
    let sharing be our religion,
    let praising be our entertainment,
    let eating be our common prayer.

O Bread of Life
    be nourishment to us.

112

Lady, in spite of all buffeting
    I hold tight to you.

In spite of all differing opinions
    I hold tight to you.

In spite of all evidence and argument
    I hold tight to you.

In spite of all persecution
    I hold tight to you.

In spite of wisdom, cynicism, mockery,
    I hold tight to you.

Letting all others go their own way
    I hold tight to you.

Like a child in the darkness,
    I hold tight to you.

Hold tight to me in the darkness,
    Mother of life.

113

O Thou,

What do you have to fear from us,
    our small discoveries
    incomplete theories
    inspired insights

All we create is partial, temporary,
    contained within you
    painted on darkness
    like petroglyphs
    on the rock of ages

You have given us complete freedom
    to think any thought
    craft any tool
    design and create
    without offending you

Only our choices offend you
    turning from mercy
    hurting each other
    grasping and hoarding
    in spite of the generosity
    nature exemplifies

We brag about how far we have come
    how far from you —
    yet you are with us
    even in the darkness
    we have chosen

Nothing we discover, create or know
    matters more than
    these eyes
    these faces
    the ones we love
    the one who loves us
    the One behind it all

O Thou

114

In the evening I wander into the hills,

nothing in my hands to kill with or destroy,

almost invisible, empty of desire and ambition,

I walk among beasts and insects and birds of the air

in the lavender mist over mountains where the moon rises

and the sun goes down softly like a benediction

and the first stars enter the atmosphere like guests.

On a hilltop washed by a warm wind stirring the grass

I sense the sacredness of all separate creatures,

their place together before man was created,

their right to exist in harmony with each other.

Birds beat wings scattering toward the horizon,

and the wild beasts move easily through the trees.

Insects of all varieties thread the twilight

and each inch of soil is alive with mites.

Who are we — what are we to destroy them?

How dare we pollute the oceans and the skies?

We kill without thinking what took millennia to grow.

We slaughter leviathan while fishing for sardines.

I sink to my knees and raise up a wordless song,

wailla-la-la, wailla-la-la, wailla-la-la,

forgive us, forgive us, forgive us,

mother earth, father sky, creatures, trees and grass,

may we live in harmony with all sacred beings,

or may the end of mankind come to pass.

115

It takes a crisis
    to teach us who we are,

the earthquake or the hurricane,
    firestorm, famine, war

ravaging the homes of rich and poor,
    touching everyone indiscriminately,

and afterward, out in the streets,
    we work together searching for survivors,

pull buildings off the trapped,
    risking our lives in the process,

work till exhausted, rescuing, healing,
    helping whoever needs it indiscriminately,

(forget those who help themselves
    stealing and looting — they are a minority)

through which heroic effort we become
    most godlike, most generous and most human.

Christian, Moslem, Hindu, Buddhist, Jew,
    Taoist, agnostic, non-believer, too —

forgetting race, religion, caste and creed,
    we worship God by serving those in need.

116

O Lord, I am tired tonight.

No prayers, no psalms, no poems.

Only the quiet stirring of new leaves

in the lilac branches outside my window

intrudes upon exhaustion with a voice

so quietly persistent I do not know

how long I have been hearing it:

Praise God.

Praise God.

Praise God.

117

Wait. Just wait on the Lord.
    He will answer.

Be patient. Quiet yourself.
    There is time.

When has He ever abandoned you?
    Keep your cool.

He is already working on it.
His preparations are immaculate.
His timing is precise. Even now
the miracle is happening.

O wait on the Lord to provide.
    Stop fidgeting.

Once you finally give up worrying
    it will be there.

Miracle after miracle sustain us
    each day of our lives.

118

don't believe in Religion.

don't believe in System.

don't believe in Theory.

don't believe in Science.

    just believe

      in you.

being with you face to face

    i see the child

hidden behind each of your faces

    O Living One

just believe, child, in You.

119

because you rejected me i am running

because i wanted you i am running

because you didn't want me i am running

because i don't understand i am running

because it is too painful i am running

because it goes so far back i am running

because there is no end to it i am running

because i can't say it can't shout it can't
       kick it can't spit it can't kill it
       can't stop it can't fix it can't stand it

i am running to the end of the world

to jump off the end of the world

because love hurts beyond words i am running

into the darkness into disaster into my death

aching for it praying for it wanting it to be

over over over over over forever father

because i love you

120

The freshness of evening rain . . .

    Surely there is no death.
    Surely we contain all time.

Emotions from lost childhood well up . . .

    Smells of wet dust and grass.
    Bronzed rainclouds over blue rooftops.

This is my Father's world . . .

    I am home again,
    the beloved child.

I spread out and melt in the rich air.

    Into the deep peace.
    Into the kingdoms of light.

Look around me . . . everyone is there.

121

O Thou, in all serenity surround me now,
late evening light on the green garden
glowing off leaves and the dark, wet soil,
majestic ice-cream skies and a full moon
suspend me in a moment beyond clock time
as I hold my breath and praise you, Living Being,
creator of all life and light and stillness,
birch leaves accompanying me without wind
and music from all sides barely vibrating
within my cells — in the air — in the universe.
O let me declare with all certainty tonight
there is no death — only transformation.
We melt into the flow and are not destroyed
but mingled in company with iridescent souls.

122

Let us sing a great hymn of peace.

Let us sing it together in this place.

Men and women together singing of peace
    between women and men.

Parents and children singing of peace
    between children and parents.

Faces and voices of all nations and colors
    in our colorful costumes
    in our beautiful languages
    singing together one hymn
    of peace between nations
    peace between all colors

Hands holding hands across barriers and borders
    minds touching minds without
    barrier or border
    without fear
    as we sing it together

An end to all violence, to warfare and weapons,
    tired of killing
    we stand up together
    and sing this great hymn of peace

Hear us singing all over the world together
    for one day and one night
    in tight, close, spontaneous

        HARMONY

    lulling and breathing it
    sharing and daring it
    dreaming, creating it

PEACE   PEACE

ONE DAY OF PEACE IN THE WORLD

O let us sing it in praise of all life
    the great hymn of peace
    of living together
    in peace, peace,
    living together
    in peace.

123

It is not enough to bring children into the world.

> Getting pregnant is natural and easy.
> Then comes the yoke of commitment.

It is not enough to save the unborn from murder.

> We must continue to save them
> each day of their lives.

In anger we pressure these pregnant children.

> Don't kill your baby, we cry!
> Don't be a murderer!

Where are we then, when these mothers give birth?

> Do we live with them day after day
> in poverty, in hopeless conditions?

Do we convince the fathers also to stay and support?

> Do we teach them the honor of parenting,
> its great duty and joyful rewards?

Where did these children learn to abandon their children?

> They learned it from us — in our houses,
> our streets and our churches we taught them.

How can we teach them the rest of the gospel of peace?

> With mercy, forbearance, compassion,
> by example in our own daily living.

O you without sin in your shadow, cast the first stone.

124

O LET ME PRAISE YOU, LIVING LORD, FOR YOUR GOODNESS!

PRAISE YOU for being close to me in all situations!

PRAISE YOU for guarding me while I travel among all people!

PRAISE YOU for the vision of all races mingling in airports.

PRAISE YOU for the glorious testament of walls coming down!

PRAISE YOU for your name spoken in all languages!

PRAISE YOU so many believers living out their faith!

PRAISE YOU for the unspoken witness of the ovens at Dachau!

PRAISE YOU for the restoration of bombed-out cathedrals.

PRAISE YOU for the hope of release for all hostages!

PRAISE YOU for living among all the people of the world!

PRAISE YOU for the calming power of all scriptures!

PRAISE YOU for blessing us with serenity and beauty!

PRAISE YOU for bringing us back to the ones we love!

PRAISE YOU for being my companion each day and night!

PRAISE YOU for renewing each moment your promise of Peace!

125

Tomorrow will pass
and the next day will pass,
a year and several years pass,
before you understand now FREE you are.

Free to choose each action in each day.
Free to receive the blessings of the Lord.
Free to turn away and pursue your own desire.
Free to celebrate and suffer the result of your choices.
Free to return, in poverty and humility of heart.
Free to be welcomed into the house of blessing.

There is much time.
There is so little time.
The Lord has infinite patience with us,
yet little time for rhetoric and promises.

When we are REALLY PRESENT,
                              He is PRESENT.

Whatever we ask for is given, more than we need.
Whatever we are seeking comes to us in time.

The prayers of the heart are never ignored.

Choose well in your asking, your seeking.

126

sometimes chaos comes
like a storm at night

there is no joy
no hope in living

i feel the flux of
atoms in empty space

i do not see your face

lady, lady —
have mercy on me

protect me from myself
and from despair

sit with me in the boat
in the stormy night

127

I have no forgiveness unless you give it.

You have no forgiveness except from me.

We have hurt and been hurt by each other.

We both have good reasons to be angry.

The silence of our anger stands between us.

Both of us are prisoners of silence.

Silence eats up happiness like cancer.

Our lives go by while we stare out the window.

Lover, I can't live this way forever.

Forgiveness frees us simultaneously.

I'll forgive you if you'll forgive me.

128

I cannot escape you, everpresent One.
True living is relationship — I and Thou.
It is too wonderful for me — your nearness —
penetrating the membrane of consciousness —
overwhelming my soul with sudden brightness —
the flesh is nothing — it evaporates before you —
and I am flooded with shimmering divine Presence —
O wonderful! wonderful beyond all words!
your Presence filling me like sunlight!
I know this is how it will be when I die —
this explosion of joy, brilliant, expanding! —
overwhelming emotion, striking me speechless,
blind, inarticulate, crumbled and sobbing
for happiness, incandescent, radiating Presence.
O tiny, intimate Being, companion and friend,
from my first breath I have held on to you,
unquestioning, in confidence, loyal, true,
sharing every sorrow, agony, ecstasy — You
fill me with breath and light and life — You
dance in my heart and brain and capillaries — You
shelter me in your curled fingers carefully — I ache
to give myself, to enter you completely, to wander
in your bright Presence out of this broken flesh
swimming free as a dolphin in the great, surging ocean
of your spirit that surrounds me and drowns me completely
in light, sweet light, ineffable, lifegiving Light!

129

In all life there is one moment only —
this moment, continuous, extended
first breath to last, one consciousness
containing all growing, unchanged, eternal.

The child remains alive in the aging adult.
No past, no future — all is present at once —
and I am always growing, reaching out to Thou
in whom there is one moment, eternal, unchanging.

Not even my death breaks this growing.
I move through flesh as through a curtain
and see, for the first time, the great audience
watching each move I make with keen attention.

Then I step out of the spotlight to take my place
in the darkness, surrounded by souls, enjoying the play.

130

There is a darkness that deserves to die.

The devils laughed while violating me.

I saw no compassion in their eyes,

only malicious, brutal appetite.

Lord, my rage is cold enough to kill.

My teeth are bared, my back's against the wall.

Whoever comes against me gets it all.

If I must suffer so will they, by God.

I'll be their personal firing squad.

Strap them in the chair, I'll throw the switch.

I'll exterminate them like I would a cockroach.

Turning the other cheek is unthinkable.

What I saw in their eyes is unredeemable.

You may forgive them, Father, but not I.

There is a darkness that deserves to die.

131

When I look at these streets
strewn with old garbage,
broken glass and broken cars,
derelict men and women
sleeping in cardboard boxes,
I have a hard time
believing in anything
except brutality,
the common denominator
dividing all souls
into haves and have nots,
and I almost give up
giving a damn,
as if nothing could
help this suffering world,
except, bending over
some old drunk
to see if he's still
breathing suddenly
I see Your
face.

132

Lady, I discover you
    in common objects,
    hidden, but present,
    shell of the universe
    containing the ocean's voice,

Lady, you have always been present
    before light and time,
    in the first moment,
    beyond our minds,
    yet within our hearts,
    chanting the first syllable.

How wonderful, Lady, to find you here,
    flame of the candle,
    tongue of the bell,
    touching me, blessing me,
    heart of the lotus,
    expanding, contracting,
    heart of the world.

133

O Great Intercessor, hear my prayer

for the husband estranged from his wife

for the woman cut off from her lover

for parents confounded by children

for children who stomp off high tempered

for hatred lasting through ten generations

for isolate souls unable to touch or be touched

for violated hearts who cannot let go hatred

for friendships severed by a word

for families with no openness, no love

for the bruised heart, tightfisted, resisting

for prodigals, all of us, proud of our poverty

be a door and a pathway, a candlelit window,

so we can return to each other

so we can return to you

O Great Intercessor.

134

I never wanted to hurt anyone.

You remember how beautiful I was
      as a child? I ran
      with the others,
      painted pretty pictures,
      sang songs in church,
      feared no one, was
      cared for and loved . . .

Jesus — what happened?

I need some answers here.
      Everything's ruined.
      I feel like hell.
      Speak to me.
      Say something grand,
      like you did to Job
      on his ash heap,
      lifting his hands in the air.

Lord, I lift my hands in the air.

      Give me forgiveness.
      Give me another chance.

135

I want to take a long walk alone in the desert, Lady.
  Separate myself completely from all mankind.
    Sit on some isolate point and hear the wind blow.

I don't want to hear any voices, not even God's voice.
  Let me lie in the coldness of unspeaking stars all night.
  Let me ponder if anything is worth living for.

Let me wonder if anything is worth dying for, Lady.
  In the cold, still, clear, arid morning solitude,
    come to me with a good answer, or leave me alone.

136

One day I am full of your favor,
    charged with your zeal,

The next, I am hiding in the desert
    like a hunted dog.

My spirit slumps in a heap and
    terror masters me.

Where is the strong hand of the Lord?

I tremble in the dark hole,
    afraid for my life.

Yet even here, you feed me.
    Your angels come,

and later, after the whirlwind
    a voice in my ear:

    fear not — fear not

Fear not. Okay. I am waiting, Lord.
    Now what?

137

O Maker of Clouds
    that are always changing,
        Keeper of Sky,
    your gift to me
cannot be avoided.

Master of Souls,
    free in circumstances,
        bound in fixed choices,
    you play the music,
we dance to the patterns

freely, wanting to move
    the way you want us to move,
        each step unique, spontaneously
    perfect and naturally ours —
we become who we are.

Creator of Spirits,
    dust-bound dancers,
        I know that I am free
    to follow you dancing
in this step or that.

This work or that work,
    all work is your work,
        Shaper of Rainclouds,
    my life is your life,
however I live it.

Amen and amen,
    this is my answer!
        O Dancing Master
    I am your dancer
world without end!

138

Lady, give me daily work to do in the world.
Draw me into simpler, freer ways of living.

Let me stop being concerned with appearances.
No one will remember what I am wearing this day.

Let me give thanks for food, but not crave it.
Remind me to share my meal with those in need.

Turn my attention outward, to celebrate others,
to encourage life and not trample it underfoot.

Let me be modest, take a back seat and applaud,
do simple acts of service, cherish the players.

Stack the branches of my ambition in a heap
and burn them utterly to a fine, white ash.

Service must take precedence over self.
There is hunger in every face I see.

Let me bring happiness, comfort, kindness and hope.
Lady, give me your work to do daily in the world.

139

Sitting in a sunlit grove of aspens,
yellow leaves fallen and falling without wind,
a stillness from the beginning of time speaks to me.

Later, beside the slow river in the evening,
the voice of the water as it passes over the rocks,
enters my body like an ancient mother's voice.

And now, a splendor of bright stars behind branches,
after the fire's dramatic flaring finishes,
the long rest, the deep peace, the amen.

Let all that is within me praise your holy name.

140

I will sing a love song to the Lord.
O soul within me, sing for love of him.
Do not stop singing, though you are afraid.
The wild dogs will never touch you here.

Great, generous friend, merciful, Living Being,
How easily you supply all things I need.
The deep joy in my heart — the peace I want —
comes in the midst of trouble, calming me down.

Like a hidden bird, my soul will sing this song,
Praising the One who has never abandoned me,
who never quit loving, no matter what words I said,
who never quit seeking, no matter how far I strayed,

141

O Thou, you are so close to me,
even if I have no words to say,
no thoughts to grasp you with,
I feel you present here.

You know my changing heart,
confounded with contradictions,
blowing this way and that like a banner
with you as my center pole.

It isn't fashionable to love you.
I am expected to cultivate skepticism.
Yet I have known you since birth.
How could I abandon you?

The pious make demands on you as well.
You must fit into their pigeonhole.
But how can anyone know you completely?
You are a universe of faces.

I ask nothing of you,
except to feel you here with me,
and know that I am part of you
now and always, O Thou.

142

In the garden I see you, Lord.
You are walking with your friends,
picking grapes and talking softly together.
You look over and smile at me.
You have my father's face.

And now I see you healing the blind man
and talking to the woman accused of adultery
and blessing small children who cling to you.
You have my mother's face.

Then I am alone in the boat at night
in the howling wind with water splashing in
and I am afraid of drowning — and you appear! —
the sea subsides and I am not afraid.
Yours is the face of my best friend.

And now in the garden at night
they take you with clubs and torches,
accuse you, condemn you, spit in your face,
scourge you and jam a thorn-crown on your head,
drive you through scornful, jeering streets,
nail you down and lift you up to die.
You lift your bleeding face and look at me.
It is the face of my worst enemy.

Beloved One — so I have crucified you —
shouting for your death and calling it justice.
Yet you forgive me, though I deserve nothing.
You welcome a sinner like me into your kingdom.
What can I do in the face of such love,
but forgive every face that I meet.

143

and when my death arrives
like a messenger in the night
to lead me into brightness
out of this dull house
let me not fear
but grasp his hands
and eagerly set forth
into whatever is prepared.

so i entered this life
with a loud shout
taking it breath by breath
trusting others
expecting nothing
but love to last forever.

beginnings and endings
are beyond me
like a storm on the sea
that drives a ship
from one shore to another.

when my death arrives
what can i do
but climb aboard
wave to those behind
look out toward the horizon
cast off my final breath
and set forth?

144

We find what we are seeking, Lady.
We seek the desire of our heart
and, lo, it is given to us.

Lady, I have desired beauty.
I yearn for love that does not die.
I want to know the truth.

I have found beauty in the earth, Lady.
I have found love in the face of my wife
and in the eyes of my children.

I have found truth has a hard surface,
an edge that cuts through appearances,
and a frightening, blank coldness.

Truth also has a face, Lady.
The face I confront in the mirror,
questioning and searching me.

I come to an end of my seeking.
Lady, as I come to an end of my life,
I praise you for what I have found.

145

O Thou, I praise you for all you have created.
    for the universe I was born into,
    for the beauty I celebrate without understanding,
    for things in the sky, for atmospheres and clouds,
    for all that is given and works without thinking.

I praise you for the gift of water,
    for clear rain drops and crystalline snows,
    for seepage between sandgrains and through soils,
    for capillaries of liquid merging with strong streams,
    for the music water makes as it rushes over stones,
    for tumbling, boisterous, powerful, muscular rivers,
    and for the sea, vast and unknowable as the mind,
    source of all life and poetry and power.

I praise you for the surrounding earth,
    for the challenge of open space to wander in,
    for isolate places where the spirit finds itself,
    for wide stretches beaten down by the wind,
    for secret mountain canyon hideaways.
    for grit of soil and grain of rock underfoot.
    for roots of all sorts holding it all together.

I praise you for all the days of my life,
    for mornings shimmering with quiet promise,
    for evenings of tired, accomplished, reflective light,
    and deep night with its restful, processing darkness,
    for seasons that challenge me always with their changes,
    for the lifegiving, generous sun we circle around
    and the infinite, curved space continuously expanding,
    where this tiny stone, earth emerald, is spinning.

I praise you for expressing yourself so richly,
    in the starformed structures, stable and complex,
    in evolving forces tied together by tension,
    in dependent processes continuously making new life,
    in a burst of diversity, celebrating always with newness,
    in cycles that heal, returning allthings to the source.

I praise you for allthings known and unknown around me.
    for continuous generous giving forgiving life,
        for calm, mothering death in its time,
            I give you praise
            O Thou.

146

What have I left unspoken?

Who have I forgotten to pray for?

Hear them, these prayers of my heart.

Receive these wayward, prodigal voices.

Forgive my arrogant presumptions.

Soothe my unsatisfied longings.

Let there be peace between us.

Let me come home.

147

Lady, the tanks are coming into town,
along with soldiers and paratroopers.
The people who have no weapons are running
and they are gunning them down again.
Everyone follows his orders,
no one is particularly to blame.
It's just the way we are,
the way we've always been.

Lady, I hate the way we are,
the way we have always been.
I see only faces, beautiful faces,
the stricken eyes of young children
whose parents have been shot,
who understand nothing
and take it all in
through eyes that are open pools
of anger and pain.

Lady, why do we lie to each other?
Why do we fly flags in the air?
Why do we make promises of free speech
when we mean soldiers and tanks?
How can we always justify killing people
but never justify leaving them alone?
How can I get through the daily routine
knowing what I do about tanks and soldiers?

Lady, transform the way we are.
If we are to survive here together
we need to be healed of pain and anger.
We need to start saving each other,
and feeding and helping each other,
making room for free speech and ideas.
We need to discharge all soldiers
and fill all the tanks with dirt
and plant tomatoes in them.

O Lady, I ask this on a dark night
at the end of a violent century
on a ruined planet without
many chances left.

                    O Lady,

        do something.

148

O Thou, I am seeking you in the high places.
My thoughts go up like a skyhawk into the clouds.

Far from the troubled world of conflict between peoples,
far from the cities with their unending violence,
far from all traffic and mechanical noise.

O Thou, I am seeking you in the high silences of space.
I reach for you through the crashing thunderheads.

Separate me from all busyness and commotion.
Carry me into the clear skies at the top of imagining.
Let me soar on strong thermals into your holy cathedral.

O Thou, I am seeking you in the infinite field of my mind.
You are the outer edge, the boundary of all thought.

Prepare a place for me that does not change.
Open the gates of the galaxies, the doors of deep space.
Separate me into my elements like a cosmos of stars.

O Thou, I am seeking you with every thought and breath.
Be close to me each moment in my life, in my death.

149

There is one place
that is always present.

There is one time
that is always now.

There is one voice
that is always praying.

There is one face
that is always Thou.

There is one life
that is always with us.

There is one death
that is always with us.

There is one breath
that is always breathing.

We are always coming,
always leaving.

150

O Lord, when life is good
    I forget about you,

(although each hour of happiness
    is a wordless prayer
    spoken in heartbeats)

but when my sorrow comes,
    I call your name.

Forgive and do not forget me,
    prodigal Father,
    Mother maskmaker.

Love me better than I love you.
    Remember my face.

When I stand on the cold platform
    of separated souls,

    O watch for me.

    Take me home.

TRIPTYCH

An Altarpiece
For the End of the Century
by

HARALD WYNDHAM